Please return or renew this item before the latest date shown below

Renewals can be made

by internet   www.fifedirect.org.uk/libraries
in person   at any library in Fife
by phone   08451 55 00 66

Fife
C O U N C I L

Thank you for using your library

Hillary CLINTON

Michael Burgan

Raintree is an imprint of Capstone Global Library Limited, a company incorporated in England and Wales having its registered office at 7 Pilgrim Street, London, EC4V 6LB – Registered company number: 6695582

www.raintreepublishers.co.uk
myorders@raintreepublishers.co.uk

Edited by Nick Hunter, Abby Colich, and James Benefield
Designed by Philippa Jenkins
Picture research by Ruth Blair
Production by Helen McCreath
Originated by Capstone Global Library
Printed and bound in China by Leo Paper Group

ISBN 978 1 406 27394 6
17 16 15 14 13
10 9 8 7 6 5 4 3 2 1

British Library Cataloguing in Publication Data
A full catalogue record for this book is available from the British Library.

Acknowledgements
We would like to thank the following for permission to reproduce photographs: Corbis: p. 15 (© Bettmann);Getty Images: pp. 4 (Paula Bronstein), 5 (TIM CLARY/ AFP), 6 (Tim Boyle), 7 (Paul Schutzer// Time Life Pictures), 8 (Hulton Archive), 9 (Lee Balterman/Time & Life Pictures), 11 (Keystone), 12 (Cynthia Johnson/Time Life Pictures), 13 (Allan Tannenbaum/ Time Life Pictures), 14 (TIM CLARY/ AFP), 16 (CBS Photo Archive), 17 (TIM CLARY/AFP), 18 (TIM CLARY/AFP), 19 (FPG), 20 (Dirck Halstead/Time Life Pictures), 21 (Ron Sachs/Consolidated News Pictures), 22 (Mario Tama), 23 (Chris Hondros/Newsmakers), 24 (Rex Banner), 25 (Hulton Archive), 26 (TIM SLOAN/ AFP), 27 (TIM SLOAN/AFP), 28 (Robert Giroux), 29 (Jennifer S. Altman/WireImage), 30 (Scott Nelson), 31 (Scott Barbour), 32 (Mark Wilson), 33 (TED ALJIBE/ AFP), 34 (William Thomas Cain), 35 (Mel Finkelstein/NY Daily News Archive), 36 (Scott Olson), 37 (Kaveh Kazemi), 39 (Feng Li), 40 (Peter Macdiarmid), 41 (KEVIN LAMARQUE/AFP), 42 (John Moore), 43 (Chip Somodevilla); Shutterstock: p. 10 (© Pete Spiro).

Cover photograph of Hillary Clinton reproduced with permission from Getty Images (SAUL LOEB/AFP).

CONTENTS

Madame secretary

By a lake in Yangon, Burma (Myanmar), in December 2011, Hillary Clinton finally met one of her heroes. Aung San Suu Kyi had fought for decades to bring democracy to Burma. Clinton strongly supported her efforts.

The military rulers of Burma opposed Suu Kyi and sent her to jail several times for promoting democracy. These jailings created tension between Burma and the United States. But by 2011 Suu Kyi was free, and Clinton was hoping to improve ties between the United States and Burma.

Aung San Suu Kyi won a Nobel Peace Prize for her political work in Burma, which is called Myanmar by its government.

Clinton was the first US secretary of state to visit the country in more than 50 years. Clinton worked for President Barack Obama, representing the United States around the world. She won high praise for her work, and Americans consistently named her the woman they most admired.

Difficult years

But Clinton's life in the public eye had not started so well. When her husband Bill was governor of the state of Arkansas, Hillary didn't fit in with the people there. When Bill became president in 1992, Hillary came across as stubborn and quick to anger.

By 2000, though, Hillary had won support from many Americans. That year, she was elected to the US Senate. Both in the Senate and later as secretary of state, Clinton showed the world her capabilities.

Changing opinions

In 1992 Roger Stone reflected the thinking of many Republicans when he called Hillary Clinton

"grating, abrasive and boastful."

But by 2008, Clinton had shown the world her great political skills, and some Republicans supported her for secretary of state. Senator Jon Kyl said,

"She would be well-received around the world."

Learning about the world

Hillary Rodham was born on 27 October 1947, in Chicago, Illinois, USA. Her family eventually included her brothers Hugh Jr. and Tony. The Rodhams moved to nearby Park Ridge in 1950. Hillary went to good schools and got excellent grades. Her parents taught her to take care of herself. When a bully was causing trouble, Hillary's mother told her four-year-old daughter to stand up for herself. Hillary confronted the bully and won the respect of the neighbourhood kids.

Hillary first learned about politics from her father. Hugh Rodham was a conservative Republican. He wanted lower taxes and less government spending. Hillary's mother was more of a Democrat, and she particularly wanted to see all children treated well.

The young Hillary

Don Jones, the minister who took Hillary to hear Martin Luther King Jr. speak said,

> "I thought of all the youth, she was probably the most open-minded."

In high school, Hillary was elected vice president of her junior class.

Equal rights

As a teenager, Hillary learned many things about the world from her family's minister. He taught her about the hard life that many African Americans faced. In 1962 he took Hillary and other students to hear Martin Luther King Jr. speak.

THEN and NOW

Women in government
The number of women in national US government has increased from 1964 to 2013.

	1964	2013
President's cabinet of top advisers	none	4
Congress	14	98
US Supreme Court	none	3

Hillary saw political protests like this one in 1968 in Chicago.

Off to college

In 1965 Hillary left Illinois to go to Wellesley College in Massachusetts. The all-female college is one of the best in the country for women. During her four years there, Hillary changed many of her ideas about politics. She arrived as a Republican, but she came to disagree with many Republican views. Most Republicans supported the war the United States was fighting in Vietnam. By 1968 Hillary supported a Democrat for president who strongly opposed the war.

THEN and NOW

Women in college

In 1969 fewer women than men attended US universities. Some schools didn't let women attend. Today most major schools have male and female students, although some schools are still just for female students. In 2012 women made up 57 percent of students in US universities.

Hillary and her graduation speech were featured in *Life* magazine.

Politics and law

Hillary became active in politics at Wellesley and was elected president of the student union. She also spent a summer in Washington, D.C. Hillary didn't think she would ever run for a government office, but she wanted to work to make the country better. She thought she could do that as a lawyer. When she graduated in 1969, she prepared to go to Yale university, which had one of the best law schools.

BREAKING BOUNDARIES

SPEAKING OUT

An excellent student at Wellesley, Hillary was chosen to speak when her class graduated. She was the first student speaker in the school's history. She said students were "exploring a world that none of us even understands" and trying to create a better world despite "uncertainty."

Becoming a lawyer

At Yale Hillary continued to do well in the classroom. When not in school, she began working on issues that affected children. She was concerned that the kids of some farmworkers didn't have good housing. She also thought children should have more legal rights.

Hillary and Bill

During 1971 Hillary became friends with another student – Bill Clinton. The two soon fell in love. They shared a strong interest in politics and worked together to help Democrats get elected. They both graduated from Yale in 1973. Hillary headed to Massachusetts to work for the Children's Defense Fund. Bill returned to his home state of Arkansas to teach law. Although apart, they planned for their future.

> **Fact**
> Hillary was one of just 27 women out of 235 students to enter Yale Law School in 1969.

Hillary and Bill Clinton met at Yale.

WOMEN IN LAW

In Washington Hillary was part of the legal team seeking the impeachment of President Nixon to remove him from office. At that time the legal profession was still dominated by men. Hillary was one of just three women out of 43 lawyers investigating Nixon.

First legal job

In 1974 Hillary took a job in Washington, D.C., working for Democrats who were investigating President Richard M. Nixon. The president was accused of lying about his role in a political scandal called Watergate. For Hillary the pay was bad and the hours were long, but she loved the work. When the job ended, Hillary moved to Arkansas to be with Bill.

President Richard Nixon's legal difficulties were called the Watergate scandal.

Life in Arkansas

When Hillary moved to Arkansas in 1974, Bill was running for his first political office. He wanted to represent part of the state in the US House of Representatives. Hillary prepared for her new job at the University of Arkansas teaching law. Bill worked hard during his campaign, but he lost the race.

Problems in Arkansas

The next year, Hillary and Bill were married. Hillary decided to keep her own last name rather than be called Hillary Clinton. Not taking a husband's surname was uncommon at the time. Hillary's choice surprised many people in Arkansas, which was a conservative state. She also didn't pay much attention to her hair or clothes. Hillary was more concerned about what she did than how she looked.

Meanwhile, Bill continued his political career. In 1976 he was elected attorney general of Arkansas. He and Hillary moved to Little Rock, the state capital. Hillary soon got a job at a major law firm there. In 1978 Bill was elected governor of the state. Almost two years later, Hillary gave birth to the couple's only child, Chelsea.

As a young child, Chelsea Clinton sometimes went with her parents as they tried to win votes for Bill.

THEN and NOW

Feminism

Hillary was influenced by feminism – the idea that women deserve equal rights and should not define themselves by their relations with men. Feminism is still important for many women, who fear lawmakers are trying to deny them some of their rights. For example, women often make less money than men for doing the same work.

To help Bill's political career, Hillary began to pay more attention to her clothes and hairstyle. She also began to use his last name.

First lady of Arkansas

First lady of Arkansas

When it came time for Bill to run for re-election in 1980, Hillary helped to organize his campaign. She saw that voters were turning against Bill. Some Arkansans thought he was too young or could not be trusted. Bill lost his re-election.

First lady again

Hillary continued to work at the Rose Law Firm, while Bill planned to run again for governor. She was now a partner at the firm, making her one of their top lawyers. In 1982 Bill was elected governor again. Hillary helped him address one of the major problems in the state, its poor school system. Both Clintons were focused on Bill's career, but they always made time for their daughter, Chelsea.

One Arkansas reporter said Hillary showed "flashes of boldness" in her work on improving education.

14

With Hillary's hard work, Bill was able to improve education in Arkansas. The state hired better teachers and made the school year longer. Bill won re-election as governor throughout the 1980s, but he was beginning to think about running for US president. In 1988 he decided to wait, a decision Hillary backed. He needed more time to win support outside Arkansas.

Opinions of education

Hillary won praise for her work, but she upset others. After she presented her ideas to lawmakers, one said,

"Well, fellas, it looks like we might have elected the wrong Clinton."

But another lawmaker said,

"Nobody wanted us to look at the individual pieces and say, 'Is this really good or not'...it was like, 'Buy the whole deal because this is what Hillary came up with.'"

Bill Clinton spoke to Democrats at the 1988 presidential convention.

Hillary supported Bill when he ran for president in 1992.

Road to the presidency

Bill Clinton ran again for governor in 1990 and won easily. Then he announced that he wanted to be the Democratic candidate for US president in 1992. During the campaign, the Clintons told voters they would get "two for the price of one" if Bill were elected. Hillary told reporters, "I want to get deeply involved in solving problems."

Problems during the campaign

Running for president meant all Americans would learn about the Clintons. People found out that they sometimes had a difficult marriage. Americans also learned about a financial deal, called Whitewater, that Hillary had made in Arkansas. Some people involved with the deal were later sent to jail. As Americans got to know Hillary, some didn't like her. Many thought she had put her career ahead of her family. Hillary said a woman could have a career and still be a good mother.

Despite the Clintons' problems, Bill became the Democratic candidate for president. Hillary travelled the country to help him win support. On 3 November 1992, Bill won the election, and Hillary left her job at the Rose Law Firm and prepared to become first lady of the United States.

Bill chose Al Gore to be his vice presidential running mate. He and his wife, Tipper, campaigned with the Clintons.

First lady of the United States

To prepare for her new role, Hillary learned about the first ladies who came before her and their relationships with their husbands. She also still had duties as a mother. Chelsea was then 12, and the Clintons decided to send her to a private school in Washington, D.C. They wanted to keep her life private, so she could grow up as normal as possible. Reporters who asked to interview Chelsea were always told "no".

Although Hillary did not take a Cabinet job, Bill asked her to do major research for him, just as she had in Arkansas. This time, the subject was trying to provide healthcare to all Americans.

Hillary said she was tense the day her husband became president, but by night time they were joking and laughing.

THEN and NOW

Important first lady

Eleanor Roosevelt, wife of Franklin D. Roosevelt, helped shape the role of the first lady. She quietly worked to change laws for the country. Like Hillary, she believed in equal rights for all Americans. Since Roosevelt's time, first ladies have received more attention. They often publicly support an issue. Hillary supported many issues while she was first lady.

BREAKING BOUNDARIES

WORKING AT THE WHITE HOUSE

With her work on healthcare, Hillary became the first president's wife to take such an active and public role to create a new government programme. She was also given an office in the West Wing, the part of the White House where most government decisions are made.

Healthcare battles

Even before entering politics, Hillary had been concerned about healthcare. She believed "access to quality, affordable healthcare was a right." In 1992, 28 million working-age Americans did not have health insurance, and 4 million children lacked regular healthcare.

Hillary faced several problems. The government had a large deficit – it was spending more money than it raised in taxes. President Clinton's advisers didn't think they could find money to pay for more healthcare. And many Americans opposed the idea of the government telling people and companies what to do about their health.

Hillary told Congress that the president wanted to work with Republicans to win their support.

In 1994 questions about Whitewater added to Hillary's problems.

A defeat in Congress

Hillary's problems grew as she tried to improve healthcare. She held meetings in private as she gathered information. Some Republicans said these secret meetings broke the law. Other people complained that Hillary was not willing to compromise. Hillary tried to show she could compromise by working with some Republicans to make changes.

In 1993 Hillary and her team delivered a plan to Congress. Senate leaders decided the plan was too complex and wouldn't consider it. Hillary was upset, but she realized she had tried to do too much too soon. She had angered Americans who opposed her plans for change. Some Americans were disappointed that many people still wouldn't be able to afford healthcare.

Democrats disagree

Even Democrats didn't agree on how Hillary handled healthcare reform.

"It's just the right combination of...a woman's touch with a real mastery of the policy."

—Stan Greenberg

"Hillary believed...this is so clearly a moral good that no one can stand up and say, 'I'm going to stop it.'... There's just nothing stupider in government than [saying], You're with me or against me."

—Lawrence O'Donnell

Building a better image

In November 1994 Democrats lost control of the US House of Representatives. That meant Bill would have a harder time passing the laws he wanted. The results left Hillary feeling lost and confused. She felt she had not understood how to be successful as a first lady. In the following months, Hillary stepped back from politics.

Hillary donated the money she made from her book to charity. A recorded version won a national award.

It Takes a Village
WITH A NEW INTRODUCTION
Hillary Rodham Clinton

THEN and NOW

Women in government around the world

In 1997 the country with the most female representatives in the lower branch of its legislature was Sweden, with just over 40 percent. By 2012 eight countries had more than 41 percent women in their legislatures. The African country of Rwanda had the most: 56 percent.

Travelling the world

As first lady, Hillary still had to make important public appearances. In 1995 she attended the United Nations' Fourth World Conference on Women, held in Beijing, China. She talked about her interest in feminism and what she had learned about women around the world since becoming first lady.

That year Hillary also wrote a book called *It Takes a Village*. The title came from an African saying, "It takes a village to raise a child." She looked at ways that different towns and groups were trying to help children. During 1996 she travelled across the country to sell the book. Bill travelled often too, as he sought re-election as president. In November he won.

Speaking in China, Hillary won praise for seeking to protect the world's women.

23

Political and personal challenges

Early 1997 should have been a good year for the Clintons. Bill had just easily won re-election. Instead, a scandal struck that almost destroyed their marriage and Bill's career. An investigation of Hillary's Whitewater deal became linked to personal charges against Bill. In Whitewater the Clintons had invested money in land but the deal had several legal problems. Also, the country learned that Bill had been romantically involved with Monica Lewinsky, a young woman who had worked at the White House.

Despite her anger over her husband's actions, Hillary Clinton continued to carry out her public duties as first lady.

Impeachment

Late in 1998 the House of Representatives charged President Clinton with lying under oath about his relationship with Lewinsky. He faced impeachment for his actions. The Senate acted as a court to decide if he was guilty and should be removed from office. In February 1999 the Senate voted not to impeach him.

Only one other US president, Andrew Johnson, has faced an impeachment trial in the Senate. Like Clinton, Johnson remained in office.

Hillary also began to think about her own future. By law, a president cannot run for a third term. The Clintons would be leaving the White House in January 2001. Hillary began to talk to friends in politics. They told her she should run for the US Senate.

Race for the Senate

During the summer of 1999, Hillary decided to run for a seat to represent New York State in the Senate. The decision had not been easy. Some advisers warned her of the hard work it would take. But she thought about all the times she had said how important it was to have more women in government.

Hillary travelled to all 62 counties in New York State to meet voters.

BREAKING BOUNDARIES

FIRST FOR A FIRST LADY

With her campaign for the Senate, Hillary Clinton became the only first lady to run for and win a political office. Chelsea joined her as she travelled across New York State to meet voters. In 2012 Chelsea raised the possibility that she herself might one day run for political office.

The Clintons left the White House on 20 January 2001, and moved into a home in New York.

Going to New York

The decision, though, was not popular with some New Yorkers. Usually senators have spent years living and working in the state they represent. Hillary had never lived in New York State. She began travelling throughout the state to meet voters, but at times protesters greeted her with signs that said, "Go Home."

Throughout the campaign, Hillary learned how to be comfortable around the media. The Clintons also bought a house in Chappaqua, New York. Finally, on Election Day, New Yorkers showed that they thought Hillary would represent them well in the US Senate.

Fact
The Clintons bought a home in New York so Hillary could run for a Senate seat. Before then, they mostly lived in houses owned by the state of Arkansas or the US government.

27

In the Senate

On 3 January 2001, Hillary Clinton officially became a US senator. The Senate has several important duties in the US government. Besides helping to make laws, senators also approve the president's choices for certain government positions, such as judges and ambassadors. And along with the House of Representatives, the Senate has the power to declare war.

Rise of terrorism

War was not on the mind of most Americans in 2001. But Bill Clinton and the new president, George W. Bush, knew that terrorists posed a threat to the United States. They had struck US targets several times during the Clinton presidency. The most deadly terrorist group was led by Osama bin Laden.

The first attacks on 11 September 2001 hit office buildings known as the "Twin Towers." They later collapsed.

After visiting the site of the former World Trade Center, Hillary asked people to donate money to help police and others who became ill after working at the site.

Terrorists attack

On 11 September 2001, Hillary Clinton was in Washington, D.C., when Osama bin Laden struck again, targeting Hillary's new home state. Terrorists took control of two planes and flew them into New York City's World Trade Center. Another attack took place just outside Washington, D.C., and a fourth plane crashed before reaching its target.

President Bush soon announced that bin Laden was behind the attacks, which killed almost 3,000 people. The next day, Hillary returned to New York to see the destruction. Soon she was seeking money from the government to help deal with the damage.

Response to the attacks

After the attacks, *The New York Times* described how Hillary was working with Republicans and taking on a new role:

"While she once protested that she wanted to keep a low profile, she has suddenly agreed to burst into the spotlight...the crisis has presented Mrs. Clinton with the opportunity to establish herself as a senator who is buckling down and delivering for her fellow New Yorkers in a time of need."

Fighting two wars

In response to the attacks, President Bush sent troops to Afghanistan to try to hunt down Osama bin Laden. Hillary supported this military effort. Then in 2002 President Bush began turning his attention to Iraq. He feared that Iraqi leader Saddam Hussein might help terrorists attack the United States. Bush was particularly concerned about weapons of mass destruction, which can kill thousands of people at once. Bush said the United States might have to go to war to stop Hussein's possible harmful actions.

After US troops put a new, democratic government in Afghanistan, Hillary supported sending more troops there to keep order.

Many Americans opposed the Iraq War, and some Democrats disliked Hillary's support of it.

Supporting war in Iraq

When the Senate voted in October to give President Bush the power to use US military forces in Iraq, Hillary supported him. She said, "This is probably the hardest decision I have ever had to make. Any vote that might lead to war should be hard. But I cast it with conviction [strong belief]."

In the following months, President Bush sought international help for a possible war with Iraq. Finally in March 2003, US troops led an invasion of Iraq that removed Saddam Hussein from power. But the troops never found any weapons of mass destruction, and no one ever proved a link between Hussein and bin Laden.

Clinton and the war

The New York Times reported on Hillary's views of the Iraq War:

"Even as the war in Iraq proves unpopular with... some mainstream Democrats, Mrs. Clinton has emerged as one of the most prominent Democratic backers of the military activities."

31

Getting things done

Just before the Iraq War started, Hillary joined the Senate Armed Services Committee. Its work focuses on people who serve in the military and the weapons they use. She surprised some people by taking this seat, since they thought she was against war. On the committee, she showed skill in getting along with members of the Republican Party and strongly supported money to help the troops.

While some people called her Mrs. Clinton, the senator was often simply called Hillary. Around the world, she was so famous that people knew her just by her first name.

BREAKING BOUNDARIES

WOMEN IN THE MILITARY

The wars in Iraq and Afghanistan marked the first time thousands of American women fought alongside men for long periods. Some lawmakers opposed the increased role for women in combat, but Senator Clinton fought efforts that tried to limit a woman's role. In 2013 the US military ended its ban on women in combat.

In the Senate, Hillary made efforts to give veterans, people who have served in the military, better health benefits.

Looking ahead

In 2006 Hillary ran for re-election to the US Senate and won easily. Some people were already talking about her future. The media and other politicians assumed she wanted to return to the White House – as president of the United States.

Fact

Hillary Clinton served on several other Senate committees, including ones that focused on the environment and the elderly. She also continued to seek money for New York City to help it rebuild after the 11 September attacks.

Running for president

On 20 January 2007, Hillary Clinton released a video on the Internet confirming what many people already suspected. She wanted to be the Democratic candidate for president in 2008. She said she wanted to show that Americans are "still the most creative, most innovative, most effective nation in the history of the world."

Facing Barack Obama

Several other Democrats were already in the race, including Senator Barack Obama of Illinois. He first drew national attention after giving a stirring speech at the 2004 Democratic Convention. As the campaign went on, he attacked Hillary for her early support of the Iraq War. The war had gone badly after a good start, and it had become less popular with many Americans.

Hillary's Democratic opponents were all men. She started the race favourite to win.

The race to be the Democratic candidate came down to Hillary and Barack Obama. Both candidates had strong support. And no matter who won, the Democrats would make history, since for the first time either a woman or an African American would be a major party's presidential candidate. Americans waited to see who would win.

Secretary of state

By June Hillary saw that she could not get enough votes to become the presidential candidate. Her supporters were disappointed, but she told them to back Barack Obama. She said, "The time is now to unite as a single party with a single purpose...Barack Obama is my candidate. And he must be our president."

In the president's Cabinet

Barack Obama did win the election. As he created his Cabinet he asked Hillary to join it. He wanted her to take the difficult job of secretary of state. It meant Hillary would try to solve international problems. She took the job, feeling that her years of travelling the world as first lady and meeting foreign leaders had given her good experience.

Announcing Hillary Clinton as his choice for secretary of state, Barack Obama praised her for "an extraordinary intelligence and a remarkable work ethic."

THE OFFICE
of the
PRESIDENT
ELECT

The United States had many important international concerns. US troops were still fighting in Iraq and Afghanistan. Terrorists also still posed a threat. And the Middle East had been a source of violence for decades. The United States wanted to protect its ally Israel. US leaders also wanted to make sure that oil produced in Arab countries was readily available.

One concern for the US was Iran, a long-standing enemy that was believed to be developing nuclear weapons.

THEN and NOW

Women in the Cabinet

A US president did not have a woman to lead a major government agency until 1933. Franklin D. Roosevelt appointed Frances Perkins as head of the Department of Labour. The numbers slowly began to rise. Bill Clinton had the most women serving in his Cabinet at the same time: nine.

Travelling the world

In February 2009 Hillary made her first trip overseas as secretary of state, visiting several countries in Asia. In China she talked about an idea that would shape America's foreign policy: smart power. The United States had the most powerful military in the world, but it couldn't always use force to get its way. It had to rely on diplomacy and help other countries develop.

Getting tough with Iran

Among her travels, Hillary went to Russia, several countries in Europe, and Pakistan. She also began calling for tougher sanctions on Iran to try to prevent it from developing nuclear weapons. Some of these international sanctions came into force in 2010. They included limiting the weapons other countries would sell to Iran.

Other issues

As secretary of state, Hillary Clinton was not just concerned with war and peace. She attended meetings to discuss ways to improve the world's environment and slow the warming of the planet, known as climate change. She called climate change "one of the most urgent global challenges of our time." But the United States was criticized for not doing enough to address the challenge.

BREAKING BOUNDARIES

ANOTHER FIRST FOR A FIRST LADY

As secretary of state, Hillary Clinton became the first former first lady to serve in a presidential cabinet. She also set records for travelling, visiting more countries than any secretary of state before her: 112. In four years she flew over one and a half million kilometres!

Hillary visited China eight times, a sign of the Asian country's growing influence in the world.

Protests such as these in Egypt were called the "Arab Spring," an effort to bring more democracy to the region.

Seeking answers

Another challenge for the secretary of state was the situation in Israel. Many Palestinians there wanted their own country. But Israel resisted creating a country of Palestine. For several years the Israelis and extreme Palestinians fired rockets at each other. At times Hillary criticized both sides for not doing enough to bring peace to the region.

BREAKING BOUNDARIES

THE CLINTON LOOK

Hillary Clinton continued to attract attention about her appearance. The media talked about her hairstyle, or if she wore makeup. Male politicians rarely faced the same comments about their appearance. Hillary insisted she would dress and look how she wanted.

Trouble in Libya

Clinton continued her travels in 2011. She visited several countries in North Africa where people had rebelled against their leaders to try to build democratic governments. One of them was Libya, where a dictator had ruled for more than 40 years. Hillary said the United States would work with other nations to "support the Libyan people as they pursue a transition to democracy."

The following year, though, the situation in Libya was still unsettled. In September 2012 a US diplomat and three other Americans were killed in the city of Benghazi. Some Republicans put some of the blame on Hillary Clinton. Her department is supposed to protect US diplomats around the world. As questions arose about the attack, some Republicans wanted Clinton to explain what happened.

Although Hillary preferred to use smart power when possible, she supported US military aid to rebels in Libya.

Last days at the State Department

Before Hillary could meet with Congress about Benghazi, she developed a stomach illness and hit her head. Some Republicans claimed she was faking the injury to avoid answering questions. The injury led to a blood clot in her brain, and people realized the injury was real. Doctors were able to help Hillary get better.

In January 2013 Hillary finally appeared before Congress to discuss Benghazi. She seemed close to crying as she spoke of the Americans killed there. She said the country had to "do everything we can to prevent it from ever happening again."

The Clintons are perhaps the best-known political couple in the world.

Hillary spoke to Congress about Benghazi, her last major task as secretary of state.

What next?

Hillary decided not to serve as secretary of state again. She explained, "I've been doing… this incredibly important… and satisfying work here in Washington, as I say, for twenty years, I want to get out and spend some time looking at what else I can do to contribute."

To some people this meant Hillary might consider running for US president again in 2016. She has great experience in government and is respected around the world. Hillary Clinton didn't say what her plans were. But if she ran and won, she would once again make history.

Will she run again?

Journalists wondered about Hillary running for president again:

"After her successful term in Barack Obama's administration, why shouldn't she [run]?…it is hard to imagine Clinton willingly walking away from a public that…is now almost universally adoring…."
—Suzanne Goldenberg, *The Guardian*

"She might well decide that her legacy is secure, her popularity is intact, her financial prospects are bright, and her future lies with advocacy from the outside."
—Marc Ambinder, *The Week*

Glossary

advocacy practice of working strongly to achieve a particular political goal

ally friend or country that supports another person or country

attorney general top lawyer for a state or country

Cabinet heads of various government departments that advise a president or other leader

campaign process of seeking votes to win an election

candidate person running for a political office

civil rights rights that all citizens should enjoy, such as voting and equal treatment in public life

climate change current warming of the planet, which is partially caused by human activity

columnist person who regularly writes articles that express an opinion

compromise reaching an agreement by each side giving up something that it wants

conservative believing that government should not play a large role in people's lives; person who holds that belief

convention political meeting held to select or approve a candidate for a particular political party

deficit when a government spends more money in a year than it receives

democracy political system that allows people to choose their leaders

dictator leader who rules without any legal limits on his or her actions

diplomacy practice of trying to deal with other nations by talking and reaching agreements, rather than the threat of force

first lady title of the wife of a US governor or president

House of Representatives one of two houses in the US Congress that makes laws

impeachment process used to remove a public official accused of breaking the law

legislature part of a government that makes laws

nuclear weapon weapon that uses the tremendous power stored inside the nucleus, or core, of some atoms (tiny particles inside all substances)

oath legal promise to do something

re-election to elect for another term in office

reform improve something that already exists

sanctions legal limits on what a person or country can do

scandal criminal or otherwise wrong activity that creates problems for a public figure

secretary of state title of the leader of the US Department of State, which carries out the country's foreign relations

Senate one of the two houses of Congress that makes laws

term period of time someone holds a political position

terrorist person who uses violence to scare others

veteran person who served in the military

weapons of mass destruction weapons that can kill many people at once

White House home and office for the president of the United States

Timeline

1947   Hillary Diane Rodham is born on 26 October in Chicago, Illinois, USA.

1965   Hillary enters Wellesley College.

1969   Hillary graduates from Wellesley and enters Yale Law School.

1971   Hillary meets Bill Clinton at Yale.

1973   Hillary and Bill graduate from law school.

1974   Hillary does legal work in Washington, D.C., before moving to Arkansas to be with Bill.

1975   Hillary marries Bill Clinton on 11 October.

1976   Hillary begins working at the Rose Law Firm in Little Rock, Arkansas.

1978   With Bill's election as governor of Arkansas, Hillary becomes first lady of the state.

1980   Chelsea, the Clintons' only child, is born on 27 February.

1992   In November Bill wins the presidency and Hillary becomes first lady of the United States.

1995   Hillary gives a speech in Beijing, China, about women's rights. She also begins writing a book called It Takes a Village.

1999   Hillary explores the idea of running for the Senate, representing New York State.

2000   Hillary wins her election to the US Senate.

2006   Clinton wins her second term in the Senate.

2007   Hillary announces that she will be a candidate for president in 2008.

2008   In November Barack Obama wins the presidency and chooses Hillary to be his secretary of state.

2009   Clinton visits Asia, and will eventually travel to more than 100 countries.

2012   Hillary says she will not remain secretary of state for a second term. In December she suffers a head injury but recovers.

2013   Hillary Clinton officially steps down as secretary of state.

Find out more

Books

Eleanor Roosevelt, Robin S. Doak (Heinemann Library, 2012).

Hillary Clinton, Jean F. Blashfield (Marshall Cavendish Benchmark, 2011).

Hillary Rodham Clinton, Jill Eagan (Gareth Stevens, 2010).

Lean In: Women, Work, and the Will to Lead, Sheryl Sandberg (W.H. Allen, 2013).

The First Ladies of the United States of America, Michelle Obama and Allida Black (White House Historical Association, 2009)

The Women's Liberation Movement (Perspectives on Modern World History), Sylvia Engdahl, ed. (Greenhaven Press, 2012).

Websites

state.gov/secretary/
Visit the official site of the US Secretary of State Department to get information on the current and former secretaries of state.

whitehouse.gov/about/first-ladies/hillaryclinton
Read a short biography about Hillary from the White House, with information about other former first ladies as well.

Index